Instant Insights on...

Building a Conflict-Proof Relationship

GEOFF LAUGHTON

Crescendo
PUBLISHING

Instant Insights on ...
Building a Conflict-Proof Relationship
By Geoff Laughton

Copyright © 2017 by Geoff Laughton

Crescendo Publishing, LLC
300 Carlsbad Village Drive
Ste. 108A, #443
Carlsbad, California 92008-2999

www.CrescendoPublishing.com
GetPublished@CrescendoPublishing.com
1-877-575-8814

ISBN: 978-1-944177-73-7 (P)
ISBN: 978-1-944177-74-4 (E)

Printed in the United States of America
Cover design by Melody Hunter

10 9 8 7 6 5 4 3 2 1

What You'll Learn in this Book

This book is here to help you learn and embrace the idea that conflict is an essential part of any healthy relationship and that, when done well, can dramatically improve your relationship. You see, it isn't conflict that erodes a relationship; it's a combination of how you avoid conflict, how you then try to get through it when it finally becomes unavoidable, and the fact that very few people are ever taught how to handle conflict consciously and masterfully.

This book will change that for you.

With all the inner and outer conflict in our world - and in most every relationship - it's become more important than ever to see that skillful conflict resolution is truly mission-critical for everyone ... and for the planet. This means, in particular, mastering a high level of blending extraordinary communication skills with a highly developed ability to read people internally and externally, to be able to leverage even the most mundane conflicts into something transcendent that makes a huge difference not only for a couple but for their kids, their friends, their career, and for their community.

You'll get *Instant Insights* on …

- Why conflict matters when handled well.

- The number one cause of most conflicts that you can change, no matter what someone else is or isn't doing.

- The foundational building blocks for gaining mastery of conflict that allows you to de-escalate a conflict, so that you can actually reconnect and get something productive done.

- Agreements that will help you become a conflict resolution rock star.

- High-level communication techniques and tools that will support you and your partner to consistently co-create agreements—through conscious conflict—that will help you make your relationship as bulletproof as possible…while still making the differences it can make for each of you, your children, your career, and your world.

A Gift from the Author

I have over thirty years of experience dealing with conflict resolution, and I can't possibly detail every single trick I know to help conflict be an asset to, rather than a killer of your relationship. So I'm delighted to share a couple extra resources that will help you build on and practice what you glean from this book.

The first gift is a video class on "How to Be a Conflict Rock Star." This twenty-five-minute video gives you even more practical, nuts-and-bolts kinds of things that will help you productively use conflicts that arise. Because a picture's worth a thousand words, you'll get the pictures AND a few thousand words!

Secondly, you'll also receive a couple checklists to use to give you an even more conscious way of listening to and speaking to each other as allies rather than enemies.

Lastly, if you decide to take advantage of these gifts and claim them, you'll also have an opportunity to meet with me to look at your relationship in particular, with a Relationship Design Review that will explore how solid the foundation is for your and your partner's (if you have a partner) relationship and what might be ready to be designed to enhance and strengthen it now (or for a future partner if you're currently single).

www.yourrelationshiparchitect.com/ conflictproofrelationship

Dedication

This book is, first and foremost, dedicated to the woman who's taught me what love *really* looks like and means—over and over again—for better and for worse in the thirty-five years we've been together, my Beloved Sarah.

To my sons, Marc and Tom, who both continually show me what they learned about being conscious spouses and fathers from me ... and how they have delightfully surpassed me and filled in the gaps in so many ways.

I also dedicate this, with enormous gratitude, to all the clients I've worked with over the last twenty-one years who've shared their lives, hearts, souls, and minds with me in such a way that I've been able to write both this book and my previous one. Some of you have directly pushed me more than others to write, and for that I also give you my deepest appreciation.

To Susan Barnes, who started it all and who, all these years later, continues to be one of my biggest cheerleaders and butt-kickers.

Lastly, to Spirit, who's saved me, over and over again, while reminding me what true, unconditional love really is.

Table of Contents

Introduction

Before you read any farther, let's start with one key thing that will make all the difference in the world between this being just another self-help book in your closet that goes unread (or read with miniscule impact—just like the 527 other books you've bought) and it being a resource that elevates your relationship from average or OK to extraordinary. That key thing? You deciding you're ready to both embrace and let go of pain while actually doing (and being) the work.

The sad fact is that a lot of people have an unbelievably high tolerance for pain (while thinking they're doing everything they can to avoid it) and suffering. Another fact is that most people don't decide to do anything truly different until they're in enough pain and suffering. Talk about a paradox! So you're not going to get shit out of this book unless you're truly at the point where you're no longer willing to tolerate feeling horrible and/or stuck most of the time in your relationship and/or your life.

Another key factor necessary to getting the most from this book (and life) is to authentically check in with yourself and ask, "Is mundane really OK with me, or am I committed to having **the best that I can possibly have** in my relationship(s)?" You know you're actually OK with mundane if you usually stop working on your growth and evolution as soon as you're not in so much pain and suffering anymore. When this happens, you confuse the lack of pain with having truly solved the source problems and you reach that mediocre state of "We're good!" ... which usually means things don't suck as badly as they often do.

This book is NOT for people like that. So if that's your bag, God love you, but I wouldn't read any further. Anyone can pull that off.

However, if you're willing to embrace the idea that relationship (followed only by parenthood) is the best one-way ticket to spiritual evolvement, and if you are willing to take and embrace the bumps, bruises, cuts, and scrapes—and all the pain that goes with them—for the sake of your highest good, then keep reading.

I intend for this book to speak to your deepest concerns and needs in a way that you can understand, regardless of your spiritual or philosophical bent, using plain English that hasn't been dumbed down. (I do swear occasionally too, so if you're good with that, keep going.) The book will also give you practical tools that you can actually use to make a difference in the quality of your connection with your most precious loved ones, if you're brave enough to consistently use them.

Lastly, this book is for those who are steadfastly committed to having the greatest amount of freedom and happiness they can have in their life, and those who will do whatever it takes (that's legal, moral, and ethical) to live and embody that at a very high level of joy and contribution. So if you're ready to truly change your life, commit to yourself to finish this book and use the Insights to make the difference between average to extraordinary results!

Conflict Has to Become Your Friend

It's always seemed to me that your average bear (or bear-ette) doesn't likely wake up each day thinking, "Who can I piss off today?" or "What conflict can I spend the day cultivating and duking it out with someone about?" Yet because we're all human and operating from our subconscious mind about 95 percent of the time (check out Dr. Bruce Lipton's work on this) and because that mind is predominantly running an operating system, if you will, that was all put together from our third trimester in utero up to about age seven (on average), it doesn't take much to trigger all kinds of interesting reactions to things. If you add to that the general human condition that most of us have some variety of "I'm not good enough," "I'm unworthy," or some variant of the Imposter Syndrome (where you feel like it's only a matter of time before someone realizes you don't know shit about much of anything), well ... it's a perfect recipe for becoming easily upset, annoyed, irritated, or just plain highly reactive.

This can show up in what seems like the oddest or most trivial circumstances; for example, your partner asks you to please empty the trash after you're done eating and then you don't talk to them for a couple days because you're so damn pissed off at them. You know you're behaving and feeling irrationally. You say to yourself, "Dude, this is no big deal! What the hell's the matter with you?" Yet you feel absolutely powerless to do anything to change your reaction and response (known as "being triggered"). This happened to me about twenty-five years ago with Sarah.

Behind probably 95 percent of most conflicts is a wealth of unhealed wounds, stuffed upsets or distresses, and a boatload of baggage that you've not shared with anyone other than the Hall of Mirrors in your own head (not a good idea, by the way). All of those repressed feelings and communications get wound up in a ball of emotional and mental energy that lives in the body that directly impacts your physical well-being. If you keep stuffing and compartmentalizing, that energy gets stuck in your body. If you leave it there long enough, it will eventually eat you up and/or come out in very awkward ways at very awkward times, often through serious health issues and imbalances.

Conflict, like anger, is not—in and of itself—a bad thing. In fact, Dr. John Gottman, one of the preeminent scientists that has studied the science of relationship for decades, has analyzed success and failure factors that fairly predict which way a relationship will likely go. His research indicates that successful couples fight consistently, but they tend to follow some guidelines I'll share later in this book.

What gets messy and damaging is when you don't know how to give conflict empowering meaning and how to masterfully "do" it in a way that minimizes long-term and corrosive damage. So many people are horribly afraid of conflict and pain (which is understandable, given how many of us have been deeply scarred by unconscious anger) that they do whatever they can to avoid conflict, particularly in their love relationship.

However, if you consistently do that, the safety your unconscious mind thinks it's gathering up by not dealing with the conflict is illusory and quite capable of biting you on the butt in a big way. What you don't deal with—directly, powerfully, vulnerably, and honestly—will eat you and/or your relationship up! The longer that goes on, the harder it can be to heal and transcend it, and the more likely it becomes that your relationship is going to die a slow, painful death.

You need to know how to (if you don't already) hold and work with pain, disillusionment, and fear in a way that *empowers* your connection, rather than keeping you feeling so painfully disconnected by staying rooted in the fear and avoidance. To do *that* requires you to embrace conflict as a sign that you're so fully committed to having the best relationship humanly possible that you won't dare avoid it because it can lead to such a greater intimacy with your partner. If you embrace conflict rather than avoid it at all costs, the treasures are inestimable ... and often not obvious up front. You don't get to reap the best rewards without playing full-out.

What I want you to consider regarding pain— since most of us will do a lot to avoid ever feeling or dealing with it—is that if you're willing to dedicate your life to doing everything possible to not get hurt or feel hurt, then I highly recommend not having any relationship of any kind. Now, if that recommendation elicits a "WTF?!" in your mind, then there's hope for you to have extraordinary relationships and an equally extraordinary life. Why? Because there's no such thing as a pain-free relationship. You don't get one without the other. And if you're moved to try to pioneer one existing, I guarantee you're going to create way more pain than you have to have.

When you're willing to shift your perspective on pain to it being a direct pathway to growth and expansion, along with seeing it as truly nothing more than a particular flavor of energy that comes and will ultimately pass through you if you allow it to, then you and your relationships will no longer be held hostage to that particular fear. When that happens, you'll have an enormous amount of freedom, which is often one of our most important core values.

Your Instant Insights...

- Avoiding conflict to try to "keep the peace" is a surefire way to gradually destroy your relationship.

- Conflict is a sacred gift to you, your partner, and your Spirit ... if you let it be.

- Mastering working with conflict is both an art and a skill. If you're willing to practice (and life will give you innumerable opportunities to do so), you can get really good at both aspects. To get there, you also need a deep understanding of why conflict even exists and what it's actually about.

Compatibility or Bust

One of the most consistent things I've seen that leads to unproductive conflict is that most couples fail to do the front-end work early on to evaluate the potential for having a high-conflict relationship. They tend to rely mostly on emotions and love. It's so easy to get kind of hypnotized by the intoxicating blend of hormones, feelings, and sensations that are, to a fair degree, going to wear off. Lust often gets confused with compatibility. While love is a mandatory element for a great relationship, it's not enough by itself. I look at it as the ante you both have to put up to even play the game, as it were.

If you rely on attraction alone, you're going to leave out some mission-critical variables that can destroy your relationship down the road. What are some of the most important ones? While the following isn't an exhaustive list, here are some biggies:

- Risking being fully transparent and vulnerable with each other about what you want out of a relationship (including, hopefully, each of you placing a high value on transparency and vulnerability)

- Discussing what kind of relationship you really want: one dedicated to just having a good time; one dedicated to keeping each other so "safe" from conflict and dissension that you both become disciples of walking on eggshells; or one dedicated to boldly growing in ways that you hadn't thought possible and that scare the hell out of you both

- Discussing your key life and relationship values and if they are at all compatible

- Discussing each of your nonnegotiable needs and if those are compatible

- Being openly sure that, even though you feel you're in love with someone, you're both crystal clear about why you feel (and know in your gut) that you want to do it with this particular person

- Discussing what each of you prizes most for how to have fun outside the bedroom

- Having sexual compatibility on emotional, physical, and philosophical levels; and

- Discussing whether each of you wants children and what each of you sees as your likely (or existing, if you're blending a family) parenting philosophies, practices, and nonnegotiable requirements

Again, while conflict is a necessary element of a conscious relationship, there's also unnecessary conflict that's usually borne out of the shocking revelation that comes when the honeymoon phase is over and you realize that you've done the equivalent of being an evolutionist who hooked up with a creationist. There's enough truly valuable conflict available as it is, so if you can pre-emptively minimize the likelihood of setting a stage for that kind of conflict before you get too deeply into it, all the better.

Doing this requires fiercely assessing compatibility as best you can by at least asking yourself and your partner the questions above, while also creating what I would call the Constitution of the United Front for your relationship, which I'll go into in more detail in Chapter 3.

Your Instant Insights...

- Again, start with mutually sharing what kind (per above) of relationship you truly want. If your prospective partner wants a walk-on-eggshells kind of relationship and you're committed to relationship as a highly valuable growth path, you're not likely going to work out.

- Gauge up front how willing each of you is to bare your ass (not just that way) by sharing your dreams, your biggest desires in life and love, and especially your biggest fears.

- After doing this upfront work, if you're not a clear, raging "yes" to someone (and vice versa), but you think that you can commit to *hoping* that something will change ... don't do it. You're likely to regret it in the end.

Creating the Constitution of the United Front

I mentioned Dr. John Gottman's research on what characterizes the relationships that're most likely to last and those most likely to fail. He narrowed it down to four characteristics that are likely to lead a couple to a breakup or divorce:

- Criticizing your partner's character, which I call shaming your partner ("You're so stupid!")

- Defensiveness or projection ("Well, if you hadn't spoken to me in that tone of voice, I wouldn't have had to throw that plate at you!")

- Contempt ("Fuck you and the horse you and your entire family rode in on, you moron!")

- Stonewalling or deliberately (and often passive-aggressively) refusing to engage; ignoring your partner

Of these four (as vividly portrayed in *The War of the Roses*, one of my favorite movies on just about every worst-case relationship no-no there is), Gottman says that contempt is the number one predictor of divorce.

So how does one go from love and infatuation to the states Gottman describes above, other than failing to do a great job of compatibility checking in the beta-testing phase? Besides forgetting the vast importance of respect and not really knowing how to skillfully and consciously communicate, a big culprit is a lack of having what I'd call "operating principles and agreements" that you mutually develop and agree to up front, which you then periodically revisit throughout the life of the relationship. Because "operating principles and agreements" sounds like a root-canal level of corporate speak, I like the term "The Constitution of the United Front."

In effect, this is like the US Constitution. It's an actual document you create together that lays out what you're both committed to—no matter what—in your relationship that will guide you through the rockiest and the easiest of times. It's comprised of a set of clearly stated agreements that effectively guide both the rules of the road and the rules of engagement.

Rather than reinvent the wheel, below you'll find my favorite excerpts from a set of agreements developed by one of my colleagues, Jayson Gaddis:

- I agree that our marriage is designed to grow ourselves up (see Chapter 6 for more on how to work with this one).

- You are my mirror, and I am yours (see Chapter 4).

- I am committed to understanding you, no matter how long it takes me (see Chapter 7).

- I agree to tell the truth, no matter the cost (see Chapter 7).

- Win-win or no deal (see Chapter 7).

- We agree to renew, grow, and evolve in an ongoing way.

- What am I offering you? (Otherwise stated as, "What am I bringing to the table and offering to you and this relationship?")

- I will practice no blame (see Chapter 4).

- I will learn how to do conflict masterfully (which is why you've bought this book!).

These are just a few examples of such agreements that are as numerous as there are relationship experts such as myself, but there's an amazingly common set of characteristics of a successful relationship (defined not so much by longevity but by the quality and aliveness that is infused throughout the relationship in each of you) that the list above fits with quite nicely.

Think about it a second. You don't build your dream home without an architectural design and a great set of blueprints. Why on earth would you even think to embark on an intended long-term relationship commitment without having such a constitution that, I repeat, must be developed and agreed to by both of you? Once you have this strongly in place and have done your own inner due diligence to be sure that you're willing, able, and passionate about committing to it, then you're all the better prepared to deal with conflict in a whole new way, as long as you remember the foundational building blocks for mastering conflict laid out in the next few chapters!

Your Instant Insights...

- Be sure you do a reality check on how much of it is, essentially, a rehash of what you learned growing up in your family; for any element that feels like that, ask yourself, "Did this work really well for Mom and Dad?" If the answer's "no," then scrap that one and feel into what would get you back in integrity with yourself.

- Another huge variable in failed relationships is self-abandonment (also known as "selling yourself out" or settling). For each piece of the constitution, if your first truth is, "Well, I don't *mind*," rather than "This is AWESOME," or "Fucking A! This one's *outta* here," you're probably abandoning yourself already and should strongly consider going back to the drawing board.

- If you know you want a relationship dedicated to growth and evolving, learn to be self-ish so that each agreement works for you. Don't develop it on the basis of what you make up will work for your partner. Strive for ones that work for *both* of you—but not at the cost of either of you abandoning yourself.

Foundational Building Block One: The Mirror

So, I'd be leading you down a primrose path if I told you that resolving conflict is fun. It usually isn't. However, if you're coming from the right perspective, it can be an adventure. A key to making it that is to remember one crucial fact: when you're really upset or distressed (defined as irritated or annoyed, but not yet batshit-level pissed off,), it's usually all about you, not the source of the upset.

This is one of the most important points in this whole book. When you realize that, you'll learn most of the conflict you will ever encounter in your relationship is actually a conflict within and about you, which opens up new vistas for what's possible in your relationship.

Unless your partner hits you with a pan or inflicts some other kind of physical pain on you, most of what irritates you is about you being somehow out of alignment with yourself, and whoever you're pissed at is showing it to you like a mirror you can't avoid. Said another way, most upsets are about you being out of integrity with yourself and assiduously trying to avoid facing and fixing that.

For example, if you're mad that your partner isn't giving you enough attention, look at how much attention you've been giving her … or yourself. If you resent having to go to PTA meetings with your partner, are you telling them why you resent it? Are you taking 100 percent ownership for your choices, or are you effectively turning her into your parent that drove you crazy? So, before you really get into it with your partner (or even your kids), you first want to fearlessly and powerfully look long and hard in that there mirror and see what you see about what's bugging you so much about yourself.

The secret to making this effective—and, to me, this is the unavoidable truth that we *want* to avoid more than conflict itself—is to come to grips with the fact that you're 100 percent *at cause* for your experience every minute of the day, regardless of your circumstances. Most people who've gotten to live at least into their thirties know this intellectually, but I'm here to tell you this is the hardest thing for most people I've worked with to really get emotionally.

We will tie ourselves up in all kinds of knots to avoid getting this and owning it every day. Many of us operate with an assumption—often modeled to us in some way in our family of origin (more on that in Chapter 6—that when someone's upset or mad at you, the stage is automatically being set to see which person's going to be the winner and which one will be the loser. When you truly get that it's *all* about you, however, you set the stage for a strong possibility of win-win outcomes.

Now, I want to assure you that your partner, your child, and your best friend are all capable of behaving badly. My point here is not to say that you're always at fault for what's not working. (Your mind wants to go to: "Who's to blame here?") However, if you own that your feelings and reactions are *totally* in your control (especially when your ego is screaming at you that they're not) and that you actually have choices in the matter, all kinds of new options for win-win and taking appropriate responsibility will emerge. Then, blame will fade out of the picture, you'll open a door to healing wounds in you (and your partner) that you didn't even know were still in there, and you'll ultimately create more intimacy between the two of you, instead of the separation that blaming someone else for your feelings creates when you make the other person the source of your upset and the enemy.

This is not a complicated, technologically sophisticated technique you have to learn. This is simply making a conscious choice to go inside first before blasting someone else, to see what's really going on, and then using those insights to grow you, to help your partner grow (most likely), and—most importantly—to help your *relationship* grow through working out the conflict. In other words, it's where you *come from* in a conflict that will make one of the biggest differences between destruction/separation and a level of connection that builds beauty and amplifies love.

Your Instant Insights...

- A key to becoming a conflict ninja/sensei is to get committed to being fiercely and unrelentingly committed to consistent self-awareness and presence. Without that, you're essentially screwed ... and so is your partner, no matter who they are.

- When you want to blame your partner for why you're pissed or distressed, remember that *you* are 100 percent responsible for 50 percent of any relationship. So, look into the mirror they're usually unintentionally offering you, so that both you and the relationship can only benefit. Then, share what you're seeing!

- You want to be sure you have some key people (such as a men's/women's group that's dedicated to truth, no matter what) in your life that love you so much that they'll fearlessly and fiercely help you see what the mirror's revealing if *you* aren't seeing it ... and then will support you in taking what you've learned and doing something actionable to shift it.

Foundational Building Block Two:
All Is Never as It Seems

Of the many things that we hear/read/learn somewhere by the time we start resembling a real grown-up, one idea that most people struggle to understand and accept is that what you're upset about is rarely what you're *actually* upset about. Are you thinking, "Huh!?" right now? If so, that's good. Let's look at an example to help you really make sense of this.

Let's say that you and your partner are on your way to a social gathering to which you were asked to bring a gift of some kind. You're ten minutes away from arriving at your friends' house when you ask your partner, "Honey, did you remember to bring the gift?" Your partner says, "Oh shit! I totally forgot," at which point you immediately get pissed and find yourself saying something along the lines of, "What the hell's the matter with you?

How hard is it to remember a simple thing like that?"

The next thing you know, the two of you are in a fight. You walk into the party trying to make it look like everything's fine, but the other guests are muttering to each other, "Jeez, wonder what's wrong with Bob and Shirley. They're giving off some pretty funky energy!"

In your own head, you may even be saying, "Well, we're all human. It's an honest mistake, so get over it," but you just can't let it go. You're dying to get in the car to go home and really let your partner have it some more.

Sound at all familiar?

If you assume for a moment that it's really not about the forgotten gift, and if you remember what chapter 4 was all about and take full responsibility for what you're feeling (without blaming your partner), what insight might emerge that you can do something with?

To start with, you'd clearly notice what the feelings themselves are. For example, let's say you're mostly pissed off. Because being angry is about being hurt, scared, or both, you'd look at what you might be afraid of and/or if your feelings are hurt. In this example, you realize you're actually pretty afraid of what the hosts are going to think about you because you didn't bring a gift. Your mind then starts weaving a scenario along the lines of, "They're going to think we're a pair of inconsiderate jerks, this will be the last time they invite us over, and they'll post something on Facebook to that effect the next day, ensuring that we'll be known all over town as the inconsiderate a-holes of the month!" Then, to cope with how much that frightens you and to avoid feeling that fear, you just blow up at your partner and make them totally wrong and at fault for singlehandedly ruining your current and future social standing.

Ideally, you can see it's really not about forgetting the gift that's made you angry at your partner; it's about your insecurities that forgetting the gift has brought out from the deep place where you try to keep them hidden. Now, they are right on the surface for everyone to see. When you're willing to look deeper underneath the surface of things, the momentary conflict becomes the doorway to unlocking other mysteries that have gotten you easily upset or distressed a lot of the time - while simultaneously helping you practice dealing with them in a much more straightforward, powerful way. This will truly help you have more freedom and happiness in both your relationship and your life. It will also move you much more powerfully into a relationship that doesn't allow blame to ever rear its ugly head, which will make your relationship much more bulletproof.

Lastly for this chapter, I want to teach you two acronyms that will become your best friends: MSU (making shit up) and MUS (made-up shit). All humans live from one or the other (or both) most of the time. When you get upset or distressed, I can virtually guarantee you that one or the other of those is behind it.

If we go back to my example of the gift and the party and the partner that gets the most upset, you can probably see that—once they got below the surface of the upset—they'd also find out that they were making up how the hosts were going to feel or think about them once they saw there was no gift. This is not a *fact* that they'll feel that way because it hasn't *happened*. The only fact that's *absolutely* true, until proven otherwise by other facts that would have to unfold, is that the gift was forgotten. Anything beyond that is simply what one partner or the other is making up, and they're doing so from a reservoir of MUS that stretches back to childhood, where we're making shit up constantly (a habit in ourselves, by the way, that we want to watch like a hawk and break as adults). If you have some interpretation of something that's happening solely between your ears and isn't backed by objectively and mutually observed facts, you're probably making shit up that you then put in your MUS vault to use the next time it comes in handy to make you and someone else wrong.

Your Instant Insights...

- Conflict is more empowering when you look at it as a path to more deeply expanding you AND your relationship, rather than something to be feared. Follow your *gut's* direction on how to turn a particular lemon into lemonade until you get to the gifts the conflict points you to.

- When you get to understanding what a particular conflict is *really* about and you're more open mentally and emotionally, be sure to thank your partner for the gift they just gave you (whether they consciously meant to or not) and explicitly share what you can take responsibility for and what you intend to do with it going forward.

- When you figure out what an argument is *really* about, share it with at least one *other* person dear to you, what the MUS was, and give them permission to remind you if they see you going backwards with that particular issue.

Foundational Building Block Three: Who's Really in Charge?

To help you start getting the picture about why knowing this building block is *so* vital to mastering conflict resolution, I have a few questions for you:

- If you have children, how often do you find yourself speaking with them and/or reacting to them the same way that one of your parents used to talk to you ... the way that you vowed, as a kid, you'd never do when you grew up?

- In the early stages of a new relationship, how often have you found yourself getting caught, to some degree, between your partner's wants and the wants of your parents/family of origin?

- Have you ever found yourself feeling very hurt by a comment that would normally never even faze you, but in a given moment, plunges you immediately into a rage or into feeling like you've suddenly shrunk to about an inch tall?

These are some real examples that have come up in me and/or in numerous clients over the years. They're examples of not being in your right mind—which actually isn't a bad way of looking at it. Oft times, you are not in your right mind. You (and every other human being) easily get triggered into going into a child's and/or teenager's mind; however, it's not just anyone's childhood or adolescent mind that you go into. It's yours. When that happens, you're listening through a web of emotional beliefs, traumas, and disappointments that immediately take you from the present and catapult you into the past.

Everyone has what I call an "Inner Family." This consists of all the subconscious beliefs, experiences, feelings, and strategic defense systems that you've had in place most of your life that are continuing to wield more power and influence than you probably realize, until something like my above questions happens to you and/or your partner. This is most often referred to as your inner children (you don't have just one).

You never really know when these parts of you are going to get triggered (thanks to our body's cellular memory of every damn thing that's ever happened to us, whether we remember it consciously or not) and suddenly take you over. When this happens, it's as if it came out of thin air, chloroformed you unconscious, stuffed you in the trunk of the car, and then started driving the car of your life—at age four, seven, eleven, or sixteen. If you want to ensure this happens frequently, get into a relationship (or become a parent).

You can count on the fact that, until you really get to know, and feel, those parts of you—how they "think," how they react, how they feel, and how they strategically tend to respond to perceived threats of danger and emotional pain—you're extremely susceptible to behaving in a way that disregards your relationship foundation and runs amok doing whatever is perceived to be needed to get safe and to avoid pain. If you're in the first year or two of being with a love partner (married or not), you can be assured that, when the hormones and infatuation with each other quiet down a bit, you're going to meet these parts, both yours and your partner's. They are key players in what causes conflict and how to get through it in a good way.

You want to get intimately familiar with these young parts of yourself and of your partner so that you can both learn how to manage them, rather than the other way around, which is happening 95 percent of the time in your life anyway.

You'll know these young parts are in the mix because your MSU/MUS machine is running in fifth gear, a lot of what's getting made up has a very young feel to it, and you find yourself talking to your partner (if you're even talking to them) in a lot of absolutes: "You never do this!" ... "You always say that!"

When you stop to think about it, because the vast majority of our mental and behavioral patterns get programmed into us in the first seven years we're here, where do you learn how to relate to conflict? Whom do you model when it comes to dealing with conflict? That's right ... your parent(s)! (This would be the time to imagine Macaulay Culkin's face on the *Home Alone* poster.) So it can help to stop yourself in mid-argument (when you can) and ask yourself if you're really being you right now, or are you "doing" Mom and/or Dad and how they argued? (Or if you go into your cave when you're upset, which parent modeled THAT?)

Are you thinking anything like, "Holy shit! This makes a ton of sense. So what do I do with it to better handle conflicts when they come up?" Well, because this book is a short one by design, I'm going to give you a good place to start, something that you can do with yourself and your partner right off the bat. (For more comprehensive coaching on this particular set of issues, I'd recommend getting a copy of my first book *Built To Last: Designing & Maintaining a Passionate, Loving and Lasting Relationship*.)

To proactively reduce unnecessary, unhelpful conflict, you have to first be able to know when you're in your adult mind and when you're not. A simple tool for this is shown as an Instant Insight at the end of this chapter. It will also help you be forearmed, as it were; you'll have a sense of your top three biggest emotional wounds that's as brutally honest as you can muster. An unwillingness to do this, no matter how scary it is, only ensures these wounds will run you and your relationship! To give you a sample list to get started, here are some pretty common wounds that we all have:

- Nobody wants me or would love me if they knew who I really was and what I was really like. (an emotionally neglected wound)

- Don't leave me! (an abandonment wound)

- I'll take care of you no matter what, and won't worry about my needs. (a different shade of an abandonment wound that hopes to be wanted by being a seemingly indispensable partner)

- The only way I can really be loved is to do everything for my partner that I possibly can to prove I'm superhuman and indispensable. (a wound that stemmed from getting love and attention for what you did as a kid, rather than for who you were)

Once you've identified which wounds fit you and made a list of how they tend to show themselves (again, see my earlier example of the "take out the trash" incident), the next time you and/or your partner are in the midst of an upset, whichever of you is the first to realize you've "gone young" can call a time-out and say that you're going to take a bit of a breather to figure out what part(s) of you have been triggered and start to tend to them on your own; after which, you promise you'll come back to your partner to share what you learned and what, if any, energy of that upset you were able to help your young parts discharge/pass through you. Then, from having essentially "unhooked" yourself from the younger wound and beliefs that went with it, you'll be back in the present as adults, better able to use grown-up communications to resolve whatever needs resolving.

Ideally, your partner or prospective partner will do the same. If so, then you want to share with each other what you've found out. You'll likely feel at risk, scared, and highly vulnerable. However, if you're not willing to go to any of those three places with yourself and your partner, your relationship already has a potentially fatal weakness in the foundation that will make anything you build on top of it unstable and vulnerable in a way that you won't like.

Years and years ago, I learned a great tool that you can use to "talk" to your young parts that I (and my teachers) call "the two-handed writing technique." Here's how you do it:

Let's say you go to bed one night in a perfectly great mood. Your partner, however, barely gives you the time of day when you get into bed (and sure as hell isn't going to give you anything more than that), yet you don't let it get to you. You kiss your partner goodnight, and you have a great night's sleep. However, when you get up, you feel sad, a bit pissed, and just generally low energy. You also don't really want to talk with anyone.

So go find a private space in the house or outside, and take a pad and pen with you. On a piece of paper and with your dominant hand, write the following words: "Good morning, Geoff! [I'll use myself as an example.] I seem pretty upset—sad and angry. Is that true? If so, would you be willing to share what happened?" As soon as you write that sentence, put the pen in your other, non-dominant hand, and just start writing or even doodling. The words will begin to come as long as you don't try to first think what the answer is in your head and then just copy it. The trick is to imagine yourself being a conduit for that subconscious part of yourself to speak through, using your non-dominant hand.

The upset kid may "say" something like, "Well, all I wanted to do was get a hug from [partner] and she was so mean to me. It just really made me mad and hurt my feelings." Right there, you've found out that that part of you got triggered into an old wound of being ignored and/or rejected way too many times as a kid. So, with your dominant hand, you could write, "What did that remind you of? When did that happen before?" You put the pen in your other hand and just start writing whatever comes. You can then let that part of you know, through your dominant hand, that you can feel that upset and that you remember now what that was like, and you can tell them that the good news is that you're both in the present, that that circumstance that got re-stimulated will never be able to happen again, and that you—the adult—are there now to protect the young parts and the adult parts.

Now, it took me more time to write this than it takes to use that tool. What's important is that you use it consistently. It can take anywhere from ten to thirty minutes to do, but it's one of the wisest time investments you can possibly make.

If you're willing to do this authentically and build a new emotional connection with these young parts, they'll respond and let you start re-parenting them in a much healthier way than you were probably actually parented as a kid. Then, conflicts will be far less frequent and more quickly resolved ... when combined with my earlier advice that you are 100 percent responsible for your experience. Next, you want to add in *other* building elements that set you both up to win every time you get in conflict.

Your Instant Insights...

- To know if you're in your adult or your kid mind, use this yardstick: **any upset or distress that lasts more than a couple hours is not about now**. If you've gone young, try the two-handed technique to get to the heart of what's been triggered in your inner kid.

- Whatever your parents haven't or didn't ever get resolved between them, your inner children will be trying to resolve it all for them (unconsciously) in your relationships. So use #1 above to gauge whether you're in your adult or not, and then share what the current incident is reminding you of from childhood, or in the past with your partner (at an adult level) that you never resolved with each other.

- When you can identify patterns/energies that recur in conflicts and upsets that you unknowingly took on from a parent, create a ritual where you visualize (symbolically) giving that parent back that pattern, whether they're alive or not. Feel the energy being returned; feel it releasing from your physical body, and it will.

To Thine Own Self Be True ... First!

Earlier, I wrote about how one of the key elements of being a conflict rock star is the willingness to not only take full responsibility for your experience in any moment (regardless of circumstances), but to essentially have an agreement with your partner and yourself that blame is not allowed, no matter how tempting it is.

Another element that is *at least* as important, if not more so, that will conflict-proof your relationship is being an unwavering Stand to any conflict getting resolved in a win-win way, or to keep working through it until you get there. *So* many dysfunctional couples get caught in a very old destructive paradigm of where there's conflict, there *has* to be a winner and a loser. How strong that is in you will be largely determined by how you were trained.

Why do I say "trained"? Because you may have forgotten what I said earlier about how we're operating from our conscious mind only about 5 percent of the time. My coach, Ronda Renee, taught me a phrase years ago that summarized what I'd been teaching for years (in a much wordier way), and it's this question that opens up so much potentiality that can emerge through conscious conflict: "Are you operating from your truth or your training?"

I also mentioned, in the Instant Insights in Chapter 3, that self-abandonment is one of the leading causes of relationship failure. So, when you're trying to work out a conflict, you truly have to do your best to be clear on what your truth actually *is* in the matter at hand. Far too many people try to go along to get along. They withhold communications and feelings they fear will upset their partner. They fudge the facts or tailor them to what they're absolutely convinced their partner is thinking. (Remember MSU and MUS? This is a prime example of how they often come into play.) The stuff that goes unsaid rots away in each of you, usually creating more and more separation and resentment, which can ultimately take a relationship past the point of no return.

A conflict rock star will muster the courage to share what's true and important with their partner. Now, there are masterful ways to do this kind of thing, some of which I offer in the next chapter. *The key to having this approach strengthen and fortify your relationship is to **trust***. Specifically, you have to trust that not speaking your truth will likely cause (or already has caused) more damage than what you're afraid to say. You need to trust (unless you have too much incontrovertible evidence that your partner and relationship have completely lost the love element) that your basic commitment to your constitution, your love for each other (even if it seems like it's only an ember left), and your strength to be resilient (by the way, another critical element to relationship success) and respectful under any circumstance will get you through anything.

Sarah and I, for example, have endured several circumstances in the last thirty-five years that would kill most relationships, and I predominantly attribute that to our intense commitment, to how much we have always respected each other, and to our resilience. Having and maintaining a strong, immovable mutual respect for each other that's reflected in how you talk to each other is essential for relationship and conflict-resolution success. When you truly have that for, and with, each other, and when you do your level best to honor that while communicating what seem like tough truths to each other, you'll lick the fear of conflict while strengthening your commitment to using it as a tool for greatness.

Let's look at some very useful ways to communicate masterfully, in and out of conflict, in chapter 8.

Your Instant Insights...

- Keeping trust strong is essential, and fear leads to a catalog of withholds. So, to clear recurring conflicts, make a list of withholds you have with your Partner that've kept you angry or resentful. Then, drop into your heart and talk to your partner about them as if your partner is The Beloved Itself, rather than a false enemy your mind has made up.

- If you haven't taken an inventory of what your needs, desires, wants, and values within the last 3-5 years, it's time to do so. Many conflicts result from a conflict between your needs and values and those of your Partner. Then, share them with each other to start reducing unnecessary conflicts.

- When you are sharing your truths - particularly ones that are difficult to say and that may be difficult for your partner to hear - be sure you both are clear on the context and intention for the sharing up front and that you're in the discussion until it's all done (see Chapter 8 for how to do this). Take the risk of being vulnerable; it will almost always help.

Communicating Like You Mean It

I'm going to begin this final chapter by giving you the Spiritual McNugget that makes all the difference in the world to the communication outcome: communication is only successful when both parties authentically share everything they need to, when both parties feel heard and understood (meaning they feel that the other party got into their shoes and world mentally and emotionally as much as possible), and when each party realizes that the other one doesn't feel heard and understood until *they* say so. If you remember that and give your best to get there, then any conflict can get you both one step closer to greater intimacy, to clearing the air between you, to more connection, and to opening amazing potential for growth that takes your relationship to the next level. How cool is that?!

So if you're now thinking something like, "Easy for you to say, Buster … you're just sitting at your keyboard writing a bunch of stuff that's really hard to do," remember that life, relationship, and communication/conflict mastery are all practices. Let the challenge be an inspiration, rather than a red light.

Given there could be one whole book just on communicating masterfully, I'm going to give you some of the best tools/techniques I've learned over the last thirty-five years. If you use them consistently, I promise you that you will see major improvements in your relationship and greater clarity on what truly works for you.

Great communication in a relationship requires so much more than just vocabulary and language skills. So much energetic, nonverbal communication is always going on—our facial expressions, our body language, our proximity to another person during a "conversation," and the tangled web of all that we haven't communicated in the past ... mixed with God knows how many agendas present between your conscious and unconscious minds. Having great communication techniques alone will not give you the relationship you really want and deserve, so you want to remember two caveats up front when communicating:

- Actions speak louder than words.

- If your energy isn't congruent with your words, you're lying to yourself and to whomever you're communicating with;

they'll feel it, and—in that moment—you're not trustworthy.

With the first bullet above, you have to consistently do what you promise, or you're not trustworthy and promises are meaningless. If that gets to be the rule rather than the exception, you're seriously risking your relationship. So it's best not to say something that you're not ready and willing to back up with your actions and integrity. It's that simple.

Regarding the second bullet, have you ever said to your partner, "I love you," without even looking them in the eye when you did it, or have you said it on the phone while you were reading your e-mail? Either way, the other person will likely walk away from that not feeling loved. Why? Because you only said words that weren't connected to the actual things you were saying, which means you weren't present in this kind of situation. For communication to be effective, you both need to do whatever it takes for you to be fully present with yourself and the other ... body-, mind- and heart-present. In this example, the "I love you" is rote, and hearing the words, your Beloved is going, "Really?!"

Remember, too, that you have to listen as well as or better than you talk. If you're listening to your partner bare their soul to you and you're looking them in the eye saying "I understand" while your mind is thinking about what you've got to do when you get to the office, they'll be able to feel that you're not really all there because something is missing in the energy. It's kind of like faking an orgasm. It can sound great, but if you know what a real one feels like, accept no substitutes! Great communication is the combination of words, energy, congruence, resonance, body language, tone of voice, and presence.

Now, to be a masterful communicator, you're going to need to be as aware as you can possibly be of:

- Each other's Love Language ... if you know what your partner's primary Love Language is and are willing to try to deliver what you need to say including as much of their language as you can, you'll be heard more effectively. [To get a more detailed background on what Love Languages are and why they matter, as well as to find out what each other's language is, go to http://www.5lovelanguages.com/profile/]

- Your intention for communicating and your desired outcome for the communication

- What you're actually feeling about what you want to communicate

- What results you are committed to

- What you're afraid to say (so that you do it anyway)

- If you're emotionally clear enough to remember the communication has to end in a win-win

- Your body language needs to be open and nonaggressive if you want to be heard fully; if you're not able to do that, wait.

Once you're clear on the "why" for your communication and what your intentions are for the best outcome for you both (win-win, remember!), start with what's called "setting up the other's listening," which is a crucial communication skill. Essentially, it means creating a context for the other person that allows them to know ahead of time that they're safe, that you mean them no harm, and that the best way to try to hear you is to adopt a mindset that's specific to what you want to communicate. It lets them know up front how you'd prefer they interact with you.

As an example, imagine you need to have a conversation with your partner that had one central intention behind it: for you both to be much more connected to each other. Rather than allow more pain to grow between you, you want to share what's going on for you, to hear your partner's thoughts and feelings about what you share, and to use it all as a beginning to sorting out steps that could be taken to shift things.

Next, you'd let your partner know how you'd prefer they interact with you in the conversation (e.g., asking that they not interrupt you while you're sharing what you need to communicate). Then, assure your partner that you will ask them for their feedback and responses, followed by a chance for them to begin sorting out what actions could be taken to start shifting things.

It's also important that, in using this kind of approach, you ask the other person—before you launch into what you want to express—if they're willing to agree to your requests. If they are, great! If not, then come up with a different request or ask them to make a counteroffer so that you can start with a more bite-sized chunk. If the other person's a flat-out "no" and it's a really important issue to you, then gently but firmly let them know that this conversation has to happen, and if now's not the time, then ask them when in the next day or two they're willing to do what it takes to make themselves available to you. Don't give up on your needs (another useful aspect of effective communication, by the way).

There's one last thing I want to say about intention. One of the most important intentions to have is to commit to making any communication— especially when you're heartbroken or enraged— compassionate, respectful, transparent, and vulnerable. I've heard stories of two people (who say they love each other) exchanging words you'd never say to a coworker or a friend. When I press such people on why they were so disrespectful and even cruel, they say things like, "They deserved it," or (my favorite) "I couldn't help myself." To buy either of those justifications, folks, is heinous at worst and naïve at a level of "wake the hell up!" at best.

Once the stage has been set, here are some guidelines that will give you both that win-win you're each (hopefully) committed to:

- **No Withholds** – In my experience, what you don't say or haven't said is usually the kindling for burning your relationship up over time. A "withhold" is a communication (or usually a series of them) that was never delivered ... and should've been when it was up for you. So make a promise to yourself that you're going to tell the truth, the whole truth, and nothing but the truth. Will it be scary or uncomfortable? Probably. But go into it as if it's not going to be scary.

- **No Mind Reading** – Half the time (or more), people withhold stuff because they're almost positive they know what someone's thinking and going to say in response to whatever they're reluctant to communicate. This is the MSU/MUS trap. Avoid it by simply sharing your facts, whatever you may know you're making up about what the facts mean, and then share what you want from your partner. Keeping it that simple will really help.

- **No Assuming Something's Complete and Mutually Understood** – It's really good practice to explicitly confirm what you think you've heard from your partner by reflecting it back to them and vice versa, point by point if you have to. Feed back what you heard from the other and then ask, "Is that correct?" after each piece. (I prefer using the word "correct" or "accurate" over "right," by the way, because it gives the shadow ego less to grab onto to fire up into some unnecessary escalation.) Until they say "yes," don't move on to the next thing. Don't move on until each of you has said you're complete (you're both hearing and understanding the same thing and have come to a mutually agreed upon resolution.)

- **No Insistence on Having to Agree** – Some people seem to think that something's really wrong if you can't agree with each other when communicating. Remember that the first aim of communicating anything isn't to be right or to get agreement; it's to open a dialogue, to be heard/understood, and to open a pathway for you and the other person to be able to understand each other enough (and to, hopefully, empathize with each other enough) to be able to begin resolving differences and appreciating what's in common. The way to maximize the chances of this happening is to remember what communication's really about/for and that it's extremely unlikely you'll agree with each other all the time. In a truly conscious relationship, you're doing wonderfully when you can honestly agree to disagree, compromise, or simply agree to align with something you can't totally agree with.

- **No Speaking for the Other** – Make it a communications rule (some may call it a boundary) that, at no time, will you tell your partner what they're thinking or feeling and what that's all going to lead to. Instead, always speak only for yourself, no matter how well you want to believe you know someone, especially your spouse. Use what are called "I statements," such as, "When you look at me that way and talk to me with that particular tone of voice, I feel like you're upset with me."

- **No Using Your Partner as the Movie Screen for Your Projection Pleasure** – Do your best not to project on the other. The biggest barometer for determining if you're doing that is to watch how much you're using blaming and victim-type language. Again, speak for yourself based solely on your experience.

- **No Avoiding Authenticity and Transparency** – If you keep your eye on what you want the outcome of a communication to be instead of on your fears and MUS, this is simple. Be truthful and real in your communications with a commitment to radical honesty. This does not mean, by the way, that if you're in a bad mood, you get to be an obnoxious, disrespectful ass to your partner and chalk it up to practicing radical honesty. It means you don't withhold your vulnerabilities and shadow; instead, you risk letting each other know (and love) all parts of yourselves, knowing that the biggest healing technique for the shadow stuff (your "dark side") is to keep bringing it out into the light and loving it into submission. Take the risk of communicating imperfectly. The risks there are far less treacherous than those incurred by keeping quiet.

- **No Dodging Vulnerability** - To the men reading this (and for the Partners who love them), you can't view *emotional* vulnerability as a weakness. If you and your partner can't trust each other, you've got nothing to build on. Nothing says trustworthiness more than being authentically vulnerable with your heart, as well as with mind, body, and Spirit. If you're feeling like a mess inside and doing the strong, silent routine (unless you've partnered up with someone even more emotionally shut down/unconscious than you), your partner feels you *anyway*! So don't shoot yourself in the foot by lying. Take the chance to have an even stronger and more fulfilling relationship by being transparent and responsible for your own experience.

Your Instant Insights...

- Remember the main purpose of communication in conflict resolution is to ensure you're both being heard and understood, so that you can mutually work out whatever the resolution is going to be ... even if it ends up being to agree to disagree. Use this rule: you haven't really gotten your partner until *they* tell you you have!

- If you're pretty scared to communicate something, do a dry run with a friend you love and trust completely to say what they think you *need* to hear versus what you *want* to hear. It'll usually calm your mind down and make you more effective when doing the real deal with your partner.

- To be a master at conflict, you need to get rid of any perfectionist crap you have and err on the side of being *good enough* at communicating, so that fears don't stop you. Take the chance of communicating something in what might feel like a messy way for the sake of both transparency and keeping the relationship an adventure!

About the Author

Geoff Laughton, known as Your Relationship Architect, is the author of the internationally best-selling book *Built To Last: Designing & Maintaining a Passionate, Loving and Lasting Relationship*, in addition to being a speaker, retreat leader, and sought-after relationship coach. For more than twenty years, he's been teaching couples and individuals how to design and build the relationship and life they truly desire. He is also the founder of The Evolving Man men's movement, in addition to having coached hundreds of men to wake up their hearts and live their purpose more in the world. His proudest achievement is having been the husband of his wife, Sarah, for 35 years, along with being the father of two sons who grew into incredible men.

In a world where far too many people settle for what they believe they can get, Geoff and his book are devoted to teaching how to have love relationships that expand connection, healing, and create harmony with those dreams that people have simply neglected and/or forgotten.

During his career thus far, Geoff has worked with hundreds of private clients and couples; has led over 300 workshops; facilitated numerous life-altering retreats around the country for men, women, and couples; and has spoken at numerous live and online events.

Other Books by Geoff Laughton

Built To Last: Designing & Maintaining a Passionate, Loving and Lasting Relationship

Connect with the Author

Website:
www.yourrelationshiparchitect.com

Email:
Geoff@yourrelationshiparchitect.com

Phone:
303-709-1006

Social Media:
Facebook:
www.facebook.com/buildyourdreamrelationship

LinkedIn: www.linkedin.com/in/geofflaughton

Twitter: @geofflaughton

Instagram: www.instagram.com/rshiparch

Acknowledgements

I really want to acknowledge my Business & Life Coach Ronda Renee, without whose loving and fierce coaching, neither this book nor my first one would have ever happened. Thank you for helping me have a life I used to only occasionally dream of.

I also thank my *The Evolving Man* men's community for your endless support and encouragement, along with my own men's circle that loves me with truth over and over again.

Lastly, thanks to my team that keeps the wheels on the bus: Colleen Davis, Terri Williams, Walter Brown, the great folks at eVision Media, and Karen Fritz.

About Crescendo Publishing

Crescendo Publishing is a boutique-style, concierge VIP publishing company assisting entrepreneurs with writing, publishing, and promoting their books for the purposes of lead-generation and achieving global platform growth, then monetizing it for even more income opportunities.

Check out some of our latest best-selling AuthorPreneurs at
http://CrescendoPublishing.com/new-authors

PUBLISHING

About the Instant Insights™ Book Series

The *Instant Insights™ Book Series* is a fact-only, short-read, book series written by EXPERTS in very specialized categories. These high-value, high-quality books can be produced in ONLY 6-8 weeks, from concept to launch, in BOTH PRINT & eBOOK Formats!

This book series is FOR YOU if:

- You are an expert in your niche or area of specialty

- You want to write a book to position yourself as an expert

- You want YOUR OWN book – NOT a chapter in someone else's book

- You want to have a book to give to people when you're speaking at events or simply networking

- You want to have it available quickly

- You don't have the time to invest in writing a 200-page full book

- You don't have a ton of money to invest in the production of a full book – editing, cover design, interior layout, best-seller promotion

- You don't have a ton of time to invest in finding quality contractors for the production of your book – editing, cover design, interior layout, best-seller promotion

For more information on how you can become an *Instant Insights™* author, visit **www.InstantInsightsBooks.com**

More Books in the
Instant Insight™ *Series*

A Time Management System *for* Creative Entrepreneurs	Branding & Website Essentials *for* Entrepreneurs	How to Create & Build a Successful Beauty Business	Organizing Your Workspace *for* a Productivity Boost
How to be a Happy & Prosperous CEO	Taking Your Business from Start Up to Thrive in 45 Days	7 Strategies *for* Raising Calm, Inspired, & Successful Children	Creating a Solid, Lasting Connection with Your Kids
12 Leadership Powers *for* Successful Women	Motivation: Your Master Key to Success & Riches!	Performance Power: Clarity, Confidence, & Joy	Practical Natural Healing Tips *for* Vibrant Living
The Art of Selling to a Woman	Unconventional Methods *for* Writing a Best Selling Book	Defining Moments with Family, Friends, & More	Building a Conflict-Proof Relationship

Crescendo

CrescendoPublishing.com